I0814474

THE POCKET

Oxford

Published in 2025
by Gemini Books
Part of Gemini Books Group

Based in Woodbridge and London
Marine House, Tide Mill Way
Woodbridge, Suffolk IP12 1AP
United Kingdom

www.geminibooks.com

Part of the Gemini Pocket Series

Cover images: Based on an original photograph by David Iliff. Licence: CC BY-SA 3.0

ISBN 978-1-80247-275-2

A CIP catalogue record for this book is available from the British Library.
from the British Library.

Printed in China

10 9 8 7 6 5 4 3 2 1

THE POCKET

Oxford

G:

Contents

INTRODUCTION

Welcome to Oxford, Britain's most beautiful city – we can prove it, we promise – and a thrilling landscape filled with spires and streets steeped in history, mystery and victory. Around every corner, and behind every carved gargoyle, lies a portal to another time (and, sometimes, dimension), with landmarks and attractions dating back more than a millennium. In that time, Oxford has inspired and influenced a plethora of poets, philosophers and politicians of British history past, present and future, all of whom are indebted to the city's spellbinding sights, sounds and smells, each one as stunning as the next.

As enchanting as it is enticing, Oxford stands tall today as one of the world's great 21st century cities, proudly keeping one foot tethered to the past while the other strides confidently towards the future, as it always has.

It's time to put your walking boots on. We've got some exploring to do ...

I Wonderland

Seven Million Visitors

There are 76 cities in modern Britain. Each and every one of them has their own qualities to lure travellers from around the globe, and while Oxford may be extra-special, it's no different.

In September 2024, visitor statistics* showed Oxford to be the sixth most visited city in the UK, with more than seven million visitors per year, following London, Manchester, Birmingham, Liverpool and Brighton. These travellers bring with them more than £800 million of essential income for Oxford's 5,000 local businesses.

*According to YouGov data, 2024.

Narnia Business

Oxford is famed for its portals to other worlds and dimensions as two appear in the city's greatest works of literary inspiration – Philip Pullman's *His Dark Materials* and C. S. Lewis's *The Lion, The Witch and The Wardrobe*.

To visit the magical door to Narnia, head to St Mary's passage, located at the University Church of St Mary. There, you'll discover a large wooden door protected by two golden fawns that, incredibly, look like Mr Tumnus, and a large golden lion that, upon closer inspection, looks a lot like Aslan the lion, beautifully carved into the door's centre. Is this the door the inspiration for C. S. Lewis's adventures in Narnia? We think so. He would have walked past it every day in his tenure as Christ Church college's English lecturer.

*A couple of doors down from this portal to Narnia is a familiar-looking lamp-post too – another possible source of inspiration for *The Lion, The Witch and The Wardrobe*? C. S. Lewis wrote a lamp-post into the narrative of this book after his friend J. R. R. Tolkien claimed that no fantasy world would ever have something as ordinary as a lamp-post.

Medieval Murder Capital

By the 1400s, Oxford had become one of the most influential and significant medieval cities of the western world. At that time, it had a population of 7,000 residents with around 1,500 students. Between 1296 and 1348, it also had one the highest murder rates in the country – three times higher than medieval London –with a murder rate equivalent to today of 75 murders per 100,000 people, 50 times higher than cities today! Seventy per cent of murderers were university students.*

*According to *The New Yorker* in an article entitled 'Medieval Oxford's Murder Problem', March 2024.

39 Colleges

Balliol College, University College, Merton College, Exeter College, Oriel College, Queen's College, New College, Lincoln College, All Souls College, Magdalen College, Brasenose College, Corpus Christi College, Christ Church, Trinity College, St John's College, Jesus College, Wadham College, Pembroke College, Worcester College, Keble College, Hertford College, Lady Margaret Hall, Somerville College, St Hugh's College, St Hilda's College, St Peter's College, Linacre College, St Antony's College, Nuffield College, Wolfson College, St Catherine's College, Mansfield College, Kellogg College, Harris Manchester College, Green Templeton College, St Anne's College, St Edmund Hall, Regent's Park College, Campion Hall and Reuben College.

Oxford University is a huge and diverse campus spread over the city. It's so large in fact that it occupies 239 buildings that provide the 25,000 students with more than 60 hectares (148 acres) of space. That's more than 80 football pitches in total!

Unlike most British universities, Oxford is a collection of 39 individual colleges, each one with its own sense of history, traditions, character and notable alumni. The oldest college is Balliol (1263) and the newest is Reuben College (2019). As each college is important, we'll list them all here for you to memorize.

The Oxford Union

"I am humbled to be lecturing in a place that has previously been filled by such notable figures as Mother Theresa, Albert Einstein, Ronald Reagan, Robert Kennedy and Malcolm X. I've even heard that Kermit the Frog has made an appearance here, and I'm sure he didn't find it any easier being up here than I do."

Michael Jackson, Oxford Union speech, 2001

The city's prestigious debating society, the Oxford Union, was founded at Christ Church college in 1823 and has since hosted thousands of debates hosted by influential world figures, from Winston Churchill to Queen Elizabeth II, Mahatma Gandhi to Tom Hanks, to speak on topics such as: politics, terrorism, religion, ethics, pop culture.

One notable debate was human rights activist Malcolm X's December 1964 speech on extremism. As if to prove his point, within three months of his speech, he was shot dead.

The Oxford Dodo

The dodo, the infamously extinct flightless bird native to Mauritius began to die off around the start of the 1700s after European colonizers – and their dogs, cats, rats and pigs – went to town. While no one has seen a live dodo since its last sighting in 1662, the Oxford University Museum of Natural History does keep the only surviving remains of the creature's soft tissue that exists anywhere in the world – including skin still intact on a skull, and a feather removed from its head. This specimen is called the Oxford Dodo.

In their prime, dodos were one of the world's biggest birds, with a height more than 1 metre (3¼ feet) and a weight of more than 20 kilogrammes (44 pounds). Apparently they tasted delicious too.

The Clerk's Tale

The Canterbury Tales, by Geoffrey Chaucer, remains one of the one greatest masterpieces of early English lierature. Written between 1387 and 1400, the *Tales* contain 24 individual stories, as recanted by pilgrims on the long journey from London to Canterbury. One of the most famous stories is *The Clerk's Tale*, told by the Clerk of Oxford, a scholar of logic and philosophy who recalls the troubled times of Griselda, a young woman whose husband tests her loyalty in a series of cruel torments.

The Headington Shark

One of Oxford's most curious tourist attractions is the Headington Shark, located at 2 New High Street, in the suburb of Headington. The shark is a 7.6-metre (25-foot) fibreglass sculpture created by artist John Buckley that dives head-first into the roof of a house.

The artwork, installed in August 1986, was a protest against nuclear weapons, with the shark employed as a metaphor for falling bombs. "In Oxford, Spring 1986, planes were taking off from Upper Heyford and dropping their load from the clear blue sky on Libya. Our fears and vulnerabilities come this time from above," Buckley says on his website about the piece.

In 2022, Oxford City Council made the "Shark House" a heritage site for its special contribution to the community.

3 Minutes, 59.4 Seconds

The time it took athlete Roger Bannister to become the fastest person ever to run a mile on 6 May 1954, at Oxford's Iffley Road track. This world-record first is now regarded as one of the most astonishing achievements in the history of athletics. It transformed Bannister into a global sports icon and also cemented Oxford as the home of the four-minute mile. "University athletes had been trying for years and it just didn't seem to be capable of being broken," Bannister told journalists after the sprint. "There was a magic about four symmetrical laps of one minute each. It was just something that caught the public's imagination."

The Bodleian Oath

For those of you wishing to visit the Bodleian Library, you will be required to recite orally a formal traditional oath before admission.

I hereby undertake not to remove from the Library, nor to mark, deface, or injure in any way, any volume, document or other object belonging to it or in its custody; not to bring into the Library, or kindle therein, any fire or flame, and not to smoke in the Library; and I promise to obey all rules of the Library.

This oath dates back to 1602 when Thomas Bodley founded the library. For those of you wishing to swear even more allegiance to Mr Bodley, feel free to whisper his motto – *Quarta perennis* – as you enter. It means "The fourth will last forever", a reference to the Bodleian being the "fourth" library built in Oxford. Now, there are more than 100 libraries.

The Boat Race

The rivalry between the universities of Oxford and Cambridge can be traced back as far as 1209, when a group of disaffected scholars left the city, and formed a new institution in Cambridge (see p. 52). The annual Boat Race between the Universities of Oxford and Cambridge on the River Thames commences every April and reignites the competition, now considered the oldest sporting rivalry in the world, dating back to the first race in 1829.

As of 2024, Cambridge is out in front leading both the men's and women's races with 86 (men's) and 47 (women's) victories. Oxford trails with 81 and 30 wins, respectively.

With no end in sight to this historic battle of the boats, Oxford has all the time in the world to catch up ...

Sconcing

This well-worn tradition is an Oxford University undergrad must-do, and one that dates back to at least 1617. Historically, sconcing requires the downing of an entire tankard of ale or beer via a receptacle such as a shoe or anything that can hold liquids, as a penalty for failing to comply or complete a dare or task while drunk or in breach of etiquette, at the demands of peers. The modern equivalent is "Never Have I Ever" with the victim who has "never done" a particular thing having to consume a large amount of alcohol in one.

Student City

According to Oxford City Council, one in six of Oxford's 160,000 population is a university student. This makes it the most student-dense city in the UK.

In 2024, there are more than 26,000 students, of which 12,500 are undergraduates and 14,000 are postgraduates. In order to gain one of the highly sought-after 3,300 places at the university, first-year applicants face a *one-in-seven* battle to receive a place. This is perhaps why Oxford has the lowest drop-out rate among all UK universities: only 0.9 per cent of Oxford students leave, compared with the national average of 5.3 per cent.

Great Tom

Every night at 9.05 p.m. (see Oxford Time, p. 29) Christ Church's seven-tonne bell, Great Tom, chimes 101 times, one ring for each of the 101 original scholars who attended the college in its first year of founding in 1546.

Great Tom is housed in Tom Tower, designed by Sir Christopher Wren and overlooks Christ Church, Oxford's oldest, largest and most popular college for tourists, with more than 500,000 visitors annually.

The Cheshire Sundial

"When the day becomes the night and the sky becomes the sea,
when the clock strikes heavy and there's no time for tea;
and in our darkest hour, before my final rhyme,
she will come back home to Wonderland and turn back the hands of time."

The Cheshire Cat, *Alice Through the Looking Glass*, 2016

If you go down to All Souls College today, you'll be in for a big surprise. Take a look at the blue-and-yellow clock face of the sundial in the centre of the building. It's the inspiration behind the look of Lewis Carroll's famous character, the Cheshire Cat – the one with the impossibly big grin – as originally drawn by John Tenniel. If you look closely, you'll see it.

City of Authors

Oxford has been home to more published authors than any other city in the world. Several of these authors have gone on record claiming their literary works were inspired by the city's incredible history and character. Here are our favourites, and their respective literary masterpieces:

1. **Brian Aldiss**, *Supertoys Last All Summer Long* (1969)*
2. **Lewis Carroll**, *Alice's Adventures in Wonderland* (1865)
3. **Colin Dexter**, *Last Bus to Woodstock* (1975)
4. **Kenneth Grahame**, *The Wind in the Willows* (1908)
5. **P. D. James**, *Children of Men* (1992)
6. **C. S. Lewis**, *The Chronicles of Narnia* (1950-56)
7. **Iris Murdoch**, *The Sea, The Sea* (1978)
8. **Philip Pullman**, *His Dark Materials* (1995-2000)
9. **Oscar Wilde**, *The Picture of Dorian Gray* (1890)
10. **J. R. R. Tolkien**, *The Hobbit* (1937)

*The basis for the Stanley Kubrick-developed, Steven Spielberg film *A.I. Artificial Intelligence (2001).*

Richard Dawkins

Richard Dawkins is the most respected and influential evolutionary biologist in the world. His works, *The God Delusion*, *The Selfish Gene* and *The Greatest Show on Earth*, to name but three from 20, put his ideas for evolution versus religion under the microscope on a global scale in a manner that has been both widely celebrated and controversial.

In 1962, Dawkins graduated from Oxford University's Balliol College with a degree in zoology. Since 1970, he has been a fellow of New College, Oxford, and is now an emeritus fellow. As Dawkins* once so famously put it, "Science is interesting and if you don't agree you can fuck off."

*It was Dawkins who, in 1976's *The Selfish Gene*, coined the term "meme", as a contraction of the word "phoneme", the smallest unit of sound in speech.

The Oxford Revue

Founded in 1953, Oxford University's world-famous student comedy group, the Oxford Revue,* has produced many huge stars in British comedy and drama, including Monty Python's Michael Palin and Terry Jones, Dudley Moore, Maggie Smith, Ken Loach, Rowan Atkinson, Richard Curtis and Alan Bennett.

During the 1980s, The Oxford Revue Workshop was an essential hub of Oxford's comedy culture offering aspiring comedians such as Stewart Lee, Richard Herring, Rebecca Front, Katy Brand, Al Murray, Patrick Marber and Armando Iannucci the safe space to perform and perfect material in the cellars beneath the Oxford Union building. Without it, many of today's great British comedy would never have seen the light of day.

*Cambridge University has its own famous counterpart, Footlights.

Oxnaforda

Neolithic humans lived in Oxford more than 4,000 years ago. However, the settlement was first civilized by the Anglo-Saxons in the eighth century. It was they who gave Oxford its name, from the old Saxon *Oxnaforda*, meaning "oxen's ford",* the place where oxen could safely cross the river.

In 900 CE, oxen could cross the river here, allowing human settlement in the area. During the medieval period Oxford's pronunciation evolved to become "Oxenford", then in the fifteenth century "Oxford" was popularized, not long after the town was granted city status in 1542.

*Fords are parts of a river that are shallower than elsewhere and allow opportunities to cross.

Oxford Time

Oxford University's Christ Church college runs – rather stubbornly – five minutes later than Greenwich Mean Time, the watch by which Britain sets its clock. This is the result of a historical quirk that dates back to when British towns ran on their own differing time zones before 1847 and the introduction of GMT.

Due to Oxford's geographical location one degree west of the Prime Meridian, Christ Church has yet to alter its clocks to catch up, adhering to Oxford Time instead. Great Tom, the bell at the top of Tom Tower at Christ Church, rings at 9.05 p.m. every evening, as well as five minutes later than GMT for the start of lectures, the closing of college doors and services in Christ Church Cathedral. It also means savvy students can lie in for five minutes more.

This eccentric Oxford Time tradition inspired Lewis Carroll to create the White Rabbit in *Alice's Adventures in Wonderland*, a character who famously exclaims, "Oh, my fur and whiskers! I'm late, I'm late, I'm late!"

Oxford Slang

Oxford slang is a language Oxford students have devised to sound distinctly Oxonian. It is defined by adding the suffix "-er" to any word. The most famous examples being "Rugger" (for rugby) and "Soccer" (for association football)* and "badders" (for badminton), though other "-er" words became known nationwide, including "scorcher", "bounder", "rotter", "fiver", "tenner", "yummers", "brekkers", "champers" and, of course, "banter".

There are words that are specific to Oxford landmarks too. For example, "Soggers" (All Souls), "Bodders" (Bodleian Library), "Jaggers" (Jesus College).

According to *Jackson's Oxford Journal* (1899) to create Oxford slang all you have to do is: "Take any word in common use; knock the end off and add 'er'. If it should sound acceptable, it suffers no further mutilation. If it is still harsh and cacophonous, see what it will look like by striking off its head and the casual removal of an intermediate syllable."

*Yes, Oxford is to blame for the creation of the word "soccer".

Hitler's Oxford

Oxford is so beautiful even Adolf Hitler loved it. Despite being sacked during the Norman Conquest of Britain in the eleventh century and left in ruins, Oxford has remained relatively unscathed when it comes to great invasions. The Romans effectively ignored Oxford. As did Hitler when he decided to spare the city from his deadly Blitzkrieg bomb attacks during the Second World War.

During these hell-raids, cities such as York, Canterbury and Bath were targeted and suffered overwhelming damage, yet Oxford (and Cambridge) – home to much of the nation's world-respected academic libraries and artworks – did not. This is reportedly due to Hitler's command to keep Oxford intact. He had visions to turn Oxford into Nazi-occupied Britain's capital city if he successfully conquered the British Isles. (He didn't.)

Books For Miles

Oxford's first bookshop – Blackwell's – was established in 1879 and retains the title as the city's oldest surviving bookshop. It's also world-famous for another of its historic features – the Norrington Room – the Guinness World Record-holder known for being the largest single room selling books in the world. Barely contained in the Norrington Room are 160,000 books, filling more than 5 kilometres (3 miles) of shelving.

At its peak in the 1990s, Blackwell's had more than 70 bookshops. Only 18 remain.*

*Now owned by Waterstones, the last major bookseller remaining on Britain's high streets.

1040 CE

The date of construction for Oxford's oldest building – the Saxon Tower, located at St Michael at the North Gate Church.

To get to the top of the tower, visitors must climb 97 steps. Once there, the whole of Oxford unfolds before your eyes. It was also here, at the top, that the Oxford Martyrs were imprisoned before their grisly execution.
(See X Marks the Spot on p. 53.)

Four Spires

"And that sweet City with her dreaming spires
She needs not June for beauty's heightening."

Matthew Arnold, "Thyrsis", 1866

This famous poem of Oxford's "dreaming spires" emerged from Arnold's inspiration looking down from the top of Boars Hill, 5 kilometres (3 miles) south-west of the city. And while, yes, Oxford does have supremely dreamy spires it actually only has four of them: Christ Church Cathedral, St Mary's, All Saints and St Aldates.

Britain's Happiest City

In August 2024, Oxford was named the happiest city in the UK by a Shepherds Friendly's research study. The prestigious mutual insurance company analyzed 40 of the most popular cities across the country to determine which were the best for raising a family. Naturally, Oxford pipped Edinburgh and York to the post. There must be something in the water that makes Oxonians so happy. (It could be the thousands of punters constantly falling in.)

A Shot in the Dark

In March 2020, at the start of the COVID-19 pandemic, the world struggled with the notion that it may have to wait several years before a vaccine for coronavirus would become freely available. For 12 long months the world held its breath. As it did, the University of Oxford's Jenner Institute and Oxford Vaccine Group got down to work. By the end of the year, and in conjunction with pharmaceutical company, AstraZeneca, they had developed the first vaccine approved for combating the COVID-19 pandemic. Within two years, more than 2.6 billion doses of the Oxford-AstraZeneca vaccine were supplied to more than 180 countries, offering the world the opportunity to return to a (new) normal.

The Grand Café

"This year, Jacob the Jew opened a coffey house at the Angel in the parish of S. Peter, in the East Oxon; and there it was by some, who delighted in noveltie, drank. When he left Oxon, he sold it in Old Southampton buildings in Holborne neare London, and was living in 1671."

The Life and Times of Anthony Wood,
Antiquary of Oxford, 1632–1695

Believe it or not, Oxford was home to England's first-ever coffee house, The Grand Café, on The High. Coffee has been sold here continuously since 1650 and was even mentioned in the famous diaries of writer Samuel Pepys in the 1650s.

The Grand Café is now an Oxford institution for coffee lovers. The view out of the window isn't bad either. It's located near the Bodleian Library and Magdalen College.

Mr World Wide Web

In 1975, Tim Berners-Lee graduated from Oxford University with a bachelor's degree in Physics. Little did anyone know then that Berners-Lee would use what he had learned at Oxford to shape the modern world more than any other individual alive today. It was while working at Geneva's CERN (the European Organization for Nuclear Research), that Berners-Lee created an "internet" researchers could use to share information between interconnected computers. In a flash of inspiration that all of us are indebted to today, Berners-Lee then gave his World Wide Web free to the world.

Forty years after leaving Oxford University, Berners-Lee returned, in October 2016, to become Emeritus Professor of Christ Church's Department of Computer Science.

Monty Python

"If I'd gone to Cambridge I'd never have met either Mike Palin or Geoffrey Chaucer – and without those two meetings the rest of my life would have been quite different."

Terry Jones, *Guardian*, 2006

The legendary Oxbridge rivalry can be seen no more clearly than within the ranks of Britain's greatest ever comedy troupe, The Beatles of laughter – Monty Python! Within, two members – Michael Palin and Terry Jones – were Oxford students, while Eric Idle, Graham Chapman and John Cleese attended Cambridge. It is often said that the two dramatic societies of their universities – The Oxford Revue and the Cambridge Footlights – first gave the Pythons the chance to shine, and encouraged the rivalry to outdo each other.

In 2008, on the *Oxford Today* podcast, Palin revealed the importance of his university education. "Oxford changed my life ... being part of The Oxford Revue was an apprenticeship in writing and performing comedy."

"The truth is that Oxford is simply a very beautiful city in which it is convenient to segregate a certain number of the young of the nation while they are growing up."

Evelyn Waugh, *A Little Learning*, 1964

2 Town & Gown

Annie Rogers

For more than 800 years of its millennia-long history, women were forbidden to attend Oxford University. That all changed, thankfully, in 1878 when Lady Margaret Hall was founded and became the first college to admit women as members. Its most celebrated student was Annie Rogers who became one of the first female students to attend lectures and the first to sit exams. In 1920, Rogers received a first-class degree (in Latin, Greek and Ancient History), when women were finally permitted to receive degrees. Astonishingly, by that time, Rogers had been a Classics tutor at the university for 40 years.

By 1986, all of Oxford's male colleges were able to admit women but it's only since 2008 that all Oxford colleges have been compelled to admit both men and women.

Prime Numbers

"I went to Oxford University,
but I've never let that hold me back."

Margaret Thatcher, *As I Said to Denis*, 1997

Since 1742, Oxford University has educated 31 British Prime Ministers. An overwhelming majority of these leaders have been Conservative, including Rishi Sunak, Liz Truss, Boris Johnson, Theresa May, David Cameron, Margaret Thatcher, Edward Heath and Harold Macmillan.

Oxford Blue

Oxford University has its very own colour – Oxford Blue. It was chosen by Charles Wordsworth and Thomas Garnier, teammates in the inaugural 1829 Boat Race. It is a dark tone of azure. Cambridge has its own colour, Cambridge Blue, which is actually more of a spring green. Both colours have their very own Pantone classification numbers:

Oxford Blue: Pantone 282
Cambridge Blue: Pantone 557C

Today, the term an "Oxford Blue" refers to anyone who plays or has played sport for one of the University of Oxford's first teams in any sport. It is a highly sought-after achievement for sporty students.

The Pantone references above are printed in Oxford Blue and a slightly darker shade of Cambridge Blue.

Three Students and a University

"When I finished my degree at Oxford,
I went and acted for a bit. And I was appalling ...
that's now gone on for 35 years."

Hugh Grant, "Hugh Grant, for real",
Sunday Morning, CBS News, 7 August 2016

Aspiring screenwriter Richard Curtis achieved a first-class Bachelor of Arts in English Language and Literature at Christ Church, Oxford. It was here he began collaborating with Rowan Atkinson after they both joined the scriptwriting team of the Oxford Revue, the university's famed drama society. As fate would have it, Curtis hit the Hollywood big time when he cast both Hugh Grant and Atkinson in his 1994 film, *Four Weddings and a Funeral*. Curtis has worked with Atkinson and Grant many times since then, achieving worldwide success with films such as *Bridget Jones's Diary*, *Bean*, *Love Actually* and *Notting Hill*.

"What distinguishes Cambridge from Oxford, broadly speaking, is that nobody who has been to Cambridge feels impelled to write about it."

A. A. Milne, *It's Too Late Now: The Autobiography of a Writer*, 1939

Royal Mint

The first coin to be distributed in Britain, known as the silver penny, was minted in Oxford during the reign of King Offa of Mercia, the first "King of the English", and leader of a warrior tribe who dominated central England in the eighth century. Only three coins from Offa's reign still exist today.

After Offa, and throughout the reign of Alfred the Great, who ruled between 871 and 899 CE, coins were minted in Oxford with the name *Orsnaforda*, an old form of the word Oxford, on them. London's Royal Mint became the official standard in 1250.

Oxford University Press

The Oxford University Press, the university's prestigious and historic publisher, and the largest university press in the world, publishes more than 6,000 books a year. Oxford also has more published writers per square mile than any other place in the world.

Armando Iannucci

"No one had heard of Oxford
before Inspector Morse."

Alan Partridge, *I'm Alan Partridge*, 1997

One of Britain's greatest satirists and comedy writers, Armando Iannucci, is an English Language graduate of University College, Oxford. Since the 1990s, Iannucci has written several of Britain's best-loved comedy shows including *The Thick of It*, *Alan Partridge* and *Veep*.

Oscar Wilde

"Oxford still remains the most beautiful thing in England, and nowhere else are life and art so exquisitely blended, so perfectly made one."

Oscar Wilde, "Henry the Fourth at Oxford", Dramatic Review, 23 May 1885

The flamboyant, decadent and witty Irish playwright Oscar Wilde is undoubtedly one of the most notable students of Magdalen (pronounced "Maudlin") College, where he won the prestigious Newdigate Prize in 1878. A difficult student to contain, Wilde graduated with a Bachelor of Arts (with a double first) in November 1878. After graduation, Wilde wrote to a friend, "The dons are astonished beyond words – the Bad Boy* doing so well in the end!"

*Wilde was suspended for a term after returning late from a trip to Greece.

Rockin' Oxford

One of the most influential and inspiring British rock bands in the last half century is Oxford's Radiohead. Formerly known as On a Friday, the five-piece performed their first ever show at the Jericho Club in 1987, as well as their most important gig too. In November 1991, only their eighth gig, Radiohead performed seven songs to 25 A&R executives from some of London's biggest record labels. A few days later they signed to Parlophone and the rest is rock history.

To date, Radiohead have sold more than 30 million albums, with their masterpiece, 1997's *OK Computer*, selling more than seven million copies.

Advertisement in music magazine *Curfew* announcing Radiohead's change of name.

The World's University

Oxford University is the second oldest university in the world (the first prize goes to the University of Bologna, congrats) with teaching commencing in 1096, the same time as the start of the Crusades, coincidentally. Oxford University, however, is the oldest in the *English-speaking* world.

Oxford's bitter rival, Cambridge University, was founded a century later, in 1209 – by Oxford scholars, FYI – after three clerks were hanged in Oxford without a proper trial. So, enraged, the scholars decided to set up shop somewhere else.

X Marks the Spot

During his reign, King Henry VIII infamously decided to divorce his first wife, Catherine of Aragon. When the Pope refused to annul the marriage, Henry ordered Thomas Cranmer, the Archbishop of Canterbury, to convene a court. On 23 May 1533, Cranmer ruled the marriage null and void. A few days later, Cranmer pronounced the King legally married to Anne Boleyn, a move that led to Henry breaking from the Roman Catholic Church and establishing the Church of England.

After Henry's death in 1547,* Cranmer and two other Anglican churchmen, Nicholas Ridley and Hugh Latimer, were tried for heresy under the orders of the new Catholic queen, Mary I. They were burnt at the stake in the middle of Broad Street.

Today, an X marks the spot in the cobbled street where the pyres were built and the Oxford Martyrs, as they are now known, passed into eternity.

*FYI, Trinity College was founded by King Henry VIII in 1546, so an institution would exist after his death to produce future leaders aligned to his newly formed Church of England.

Capital of England

During England's Civil Wars (1642–51), King Charles I (and his cavaliers) famously battled Oliver Cromwell (and his roundheads), over Charles's unshakeable belief in his divine right to rule. Cromwell disagreed and had a desire to curb the power of the monarchy.

Escaping London, Charles retreated to Oxford with his army and turned the city into the nation's royalist capital, albeit briefly, from 1643 to 1646. King Charles lost the war, and his head, in 1649, when he was executed for high treason.

"Eastward, within a stone's throw, stood the twin towers of All Souls, fantastic, unreal as a house of cards, clear-cut in the sunshine, the drenched oval in the quad beneath brilliant as an emerald in the bezel of a ring. Westward, Christ Church, vast between Cathedral spire and Tom Tower; Brasenose close at hand; St Aldate's and Carfax beyond; spire and tower and quadrangle, all Oxford springing underfoot in living leaf and enduring stone, ringed far off by her bulwark of blue hills."

Dorothy L. Sayers, *Gaudy Night*, 1935

The Famous Debate

On 30 June 1860, at Oxford's University Museum, the now infamous "1860 Oxford Evolution Debate" was the place to be. The debate was between Thomas Huxley, a champion of Charles Darwin's *On the Origin of Species* – published a year previously in 1859 – and Samuel Wilberforce, a bishop from the Church of England, and fierce opponent of Darwin's book. Darwin himself was too ill to attend, but more than a thousand people turned up to hear the debate, with several hundred more turned away, according to eyewitnesses.

The day after the debate, and widely believed to have defeated his foe, Huxley claimed, "I was the most popular man in Oxford for a full four and twenty hours afterwards."

Thomas Huxley

The first written record of the word "Oxford" in relation to the burgeoning medieval city was in 912 CE when the town was mentioned in the *Anglo-Saxon Chronicle*, a collection of annals in Old English that chronicled the history of the Anglo-Saxons.

The chronicle revealed how Edward, son of Alfred the Great, the famed King of the Anglo-Saxons, came into possession of two of the greatest medieval cities with the line, "London and Oxford ... and all regions which owed obedience to these cities."

Tom, Dick & Harry

While the beloved English medieval phrase "Tom, Dick and Harry" refers to ordinary people in general, there was indeed a gang of brothers in the eighteenth century who had these names.

The Dunsdon Brothers – Tom, Dick and Harry Dunsdon – were Oxfordshire's most feared highwaymen. From Burford, the brothers would rob travellers and mail coaches on the road to Gloucester – now the A40 – before disappearing into Wychwood Forest, a dense woodland. During one highway robbery, Dick lost an arm and died from his injury.

When Tom and Harry were finally captured, the pair were executed and, according to legend, their bodies were hung from an oak tree on the same road on which they had committed their crimes. Today, the ghosts of the Dunsdon Brothers are said to haunt the area of Burford and in particular the pub, The George Inn, in Burford, one of the brother's favourite drinking haunts, now known as The Highway Inn.

The River Isis

Oxford city is the spot where two of Britain's great rivers – the Thames and the Cherwell – meet. The famous River Thames, which flows easterly towards London, is known and revered in Oxford as the Isis, the name given to the upper reaches of the river, which flow through the city.

The name is taken from the Egyptian goddess Isis, a deity worshipped at the Temple of Isis in Southwark, London, during the Roman occupation. While there are several etymological origins behind the naming of the River Thames, the most popular one says that where the River Thame in Aylesbury meets the Isis in Oxford – *Thame-isis* – the River Thames is born.

Queen Nefertari being led by Isis.

Keep on the 'Grass

Oxford has 21 suburbs,* all of which offer distinct sights, sounds and smells. The most well-known of these suburbs is upmarket Jericho, home to both the Oxford University Press and The Jericho, on Walton Street. It was at this now iconic tavern that influential British rock bands such as Radiohead, Ride, Foals and Supergrass got their first chance to impress. Indeed, after playing a show here in 1994, Supergrass were immediately offered their recording contract with Parlophone. Since 2012, a PRS Music Heritage Award plaque has hung in the main room, in commemoration of this momentous occasion. Supergrass bassist Mick Quinn told the BBC: "Everyone aspired to play The Jericho. Our first positive reviews came from there. I remember our promoter bursting into the dressing room after a gig there in 1994 telling us, 'You've got it!' You've got a record deal!'"

*Barton, Blackbird Leys, Cowley, Temple Cowley, Iffley, Littlemore, Rose Hill, Cutteslowe, Headington, New Marston, Jericho, North Oxford, Park Town, Norham Manor, Walton Manor, Osney, Risinghurst, Summertown, Sunnymead, Waterways and Wolvercote.

Oxford Street

London's most famous street name – out of more than 60,000! – is, of course, Oxford Street. The origin of this Roman road, and one of the major routes in and out of the city, dates back to the twelfth century when it was the key route for travellers heading from London to Oxford, 97 kilometres (60 miles) to the north-west of the capital city. The road linked Essex with Hampshire, and in medieval times was named Tyburn Road, after the Tyburn Gallows, for many centuries the primary site of execution in London for convicted traitors and ne'er-do-wells. Now it's where we all do our Christmas shopping.

Fortis est veritas.

Oxford city's motto.
It means: "Strong is the truth."

The UK's Most Beautiful City

In May 2024, *Time Out* ranked Oxford's city centre as the UK's most beautiful. The publication wrote, "The stretch of central Oxford between Broad Street and the High Street is just jaw-dropping, its medieval lanes and olde-worlde cottages, pubs and bookshops contrasting with the grandiose, honey-coloured stone buildings of high academia." The city was also ranked first, with an Aesthetic City Score of 8.39/10, by Atlas Ceramics in 2024 due to it having more than 26 listed buildings and monuments per square kilometre – the highest in the UK.

19 October – St Frideswide's Day!

The patron saint of Oxford, St Frideswide, is celebrated on this day every year – in and around Oxford at any rate. A princess, the daughter of King Didan, a ruler of Oxfordshire territory in the seventh century, Frideswide was so beautiful and so devoted to God that when she refused a Saxon prince's hand in marriage she was forced to flee to Oxford and found a monastery, where Christ Church college now stands. According to legend, the love-smitten prince followed Frideswide to Oxford, but was struck blind upon entering the town's gates, a miracle performed by God in acknowledgement of Frideswide's devotion.

In the Oxford Economics Global Cities Index 2024, Oxford was ranked the 130th best city in the world when these five factors were considered: economics, human capital, quality of life, environment and governance. Oxford is one of five British cities to make the top 100, along with London, Leeds, Manchester and Liverpool. Today, there are around 10,000 cities in the world.

"The colleges are ancient and picturesque; the streets are almost magnificent; and the lovely Isis, which flows beside it through meadows of exquisite verdure, is spread forth into a placid expanse of waters, which reflects its majestic assemblage of towers, and spires, and domes, embosomed among aged trees."

Mary Shelley, *Frankenstein*, 1818

Alice's Door

Another legendary door from Britain's literary past can be located on the door of St Frideswide's Church, on Botley Road. The artwork on the door, a carving that depicts the legend of St Frideswide's arrival in Oxford, was sculpted by none other than the real-life Alice from Lewis Carroll's masterpiece, *Alice's Adventures in Wonderland* – Alice Liddell. The door was said to be Lewis's inspiration for the rabbit hole Alice falls through into Wonderland.

Alice Liddell was the daughter of Henry Liddell, the dean of Christ Church college, a close friend of Lewis Carroll, who was a mathematics professor at Oxford at the same time as he was writing his famous fantasy tale in the 1860s.

It was on a "golden afternoon" on 4 July 1862 as Carroll rowed upstream on the River Thames towards Godstow with Alice, her sisters and her father, that the author conjured up the idea for his Wonderland with Alice insisting that Carroll must write the story down for her. He did.

£15.7 Billion

The amount the University of Oxford contributes to the British economy every year.* It's a figure equal to the GDP of a small but wealthy nation, such as Brunei.

*According to Oxford University, 2024.

"Very nice sort of place, Oxford, I should think, for people that like that sort of place. They teach you to be a gentleman there."

George Bernard Shaw, *Man and Superman*, 1903

"The first time I set eyes on Oxford was on a day in December 1964, when I came up for interview. It was one of those bright clear days we sometimes get in winter, and it drew the honey colour out of the stone buildings and set it against a brilliant blue sky, and I fell in love with the place."

Philip Pullman, *London Review of Books*, June 2011

3 Dreaming Spires

Civil War

Each summer, a number of colleges of the University of Oxford come together to wage war on each other – with tortoises! The Tortoise Fair Race tradition began in 1555 when Trinity and Balliol colleges – two fierce rivals, even today – were first founded. Now, several colleges have a tortoise.

In May, the Tortoise Fair Race begins when an 8-metre (26-foot) wide circle of lettuce is placed on the ground, with the tortoises placed in the centre. The first tortoise to eat through the lettuce to the other side wins. The other tortoises are eaten for lunch.*

One famous tortoise, Emmanuelle, belonged to Regent's Park College. Bought from a pet shop in Oxford's Covered Market in 1976, and a resident of the college for 46 years, she came third in 2013. Her last birthday was celebrated as her 119th, though in reality she was likely to have been between 80 and 100 years old. Emmanuelle died in 2022.

*Just kidding.

Einstein's Blackboard

On 16 May 1931, the famed theoretical physicist Albert Einstein arrived in Oxford to give a lecture on the cosmological model known as Friedmann–Einstein universe, at Rhodes House, South Parks Road, as well as to receive an honorary doctorate from the university. The equations Einstein wrote on the blackboard during the lecture were never erased,* and the board itself is now preserved in the collection of the History of Science Museum, just down the road. Much to Einstein's horror, presumably, as there is a mistake in the equation.

Can you spot it?

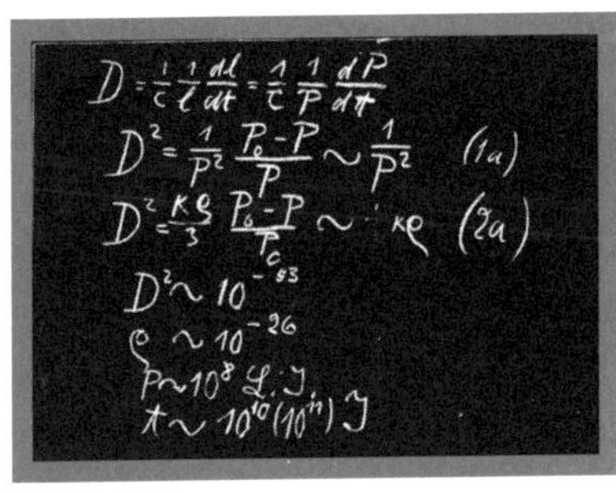

*A second blackboard of Einstein's equations, which was also due to be preserved, was accidently erased by a cleaner!

"Oxford's a complete dump!"

General Melchett to Captain Blackadder, after Blackadder attempts to reveal Nurse Mary as a German spy by asking whether her clever boyfriend "had been to one of the great universities, Oxford, Cambridge, Hull", and how she "failed to spot that only two of those are great universities", causing Melchett to parp characteristically.

"General Hospital", *Blackadder Goes Forth*,
written by Richard Curtis and Ben Elton, 1998

"The clever men at Oxford
Know all that there is to
be knowed.
But they none of them
know one half as much
As intelligent Mr Toad!"

Kenneth Grahame, *The Wind in the Willows*, 1908

Crossroads

Oxford's centre point is Carfax Tower, a twelfth-century, 23-metre (75-foot) tall belltower.

Carfax is an old English word that rather aptly translates as "crossroads", taken from the Latin *quadrifurcus*, a place where four roads meet.

Carfax Tower is also where four of Oxford's main streets meet – North Gate, South Gate, East Gate and West Gate, as so memorized in the beloved medieval rhyme:

> At North-Gate and at South-Gate too,
> St Michael guards the way,
> While o'er the East and o'er the West,
> St Peter holds his sway.

Sherlock Holmes

"And now, my poor Watson, here we are, stranded and friendless in this inhospitable town, which we cannot leave without abandoning our case."

"The Adventure of the Missing Three-Quarter",
Sir Arthur Conan Doyle, 1904

For more than a century, debate has raged as to whether the world's first "Consulting Detective", Sherlock Holmes attended Oxford University. In his Sherlock Holmes adventures, Conan Doyle only ever hints at the detective's education, suggesting he "spent two years at a prestigious university", with Oxford or Cambridge as the likely candidates. Sherlock's reference to Cambridge in the quote above suggests Oxford as the clear winner. We think.

The Inklings

Between 1930 and 1950, J. R. R. Tolkien and C. S. Lewis would meet regularly on a Tuesday in The Eagle and Child pub, in St Giles. The pub was frequented by several of the Inklings, a literary group that included a number of scholars fascinated by fantasy writing. Over pints of beer and pipe-smoking, the writers would pitch and recite their latest unfinished works for constructive criticism. It was here that both Tolkien and Lewis first read early drafts of *The Lord of the Rings* and *The Lion, The Witch and the Wardrobe*.

His Dark Materials

In 1995, Philip Pullman published the first of his three acclaimed *His Dark Materials* fantasy novels, which have sold more than 20 million copies and been translated into 50 languages. The books are widely regarded as the greatest works of fantasy of the late twentieth century. Naturally, following *Alice's Adventures in Wonderland*, *The Hobbit*, and *The Chronicles of Narnia*, the city of Oxford was an imposing influence and inspiring locale, so much so that Pullman created an alternate-universe version of the city as well. Like Tolkien, Pullman was a student at Oxford's Exeter College, before he became a teacher at a local college. He remains a resident of Oxford.

Famous Graduates

As everyone knows, you've got to be smart to study at Oxford. Many future world-changing scientists, mathematicians, philosophers and poets have passed their degrees with flying colours. You may have heard of:

Robert Hooke, MA, 1663 (coined the word "cell")

James Smithson, MA in Chemistry and Mineralogy, 1786 (Washington's prestigious Smithsonian Institute is named after him)

Lewis Carroll, BA in Mathematics with first-class honours, 1854

Oscar Wilde, BA in classical moderations and literae humaniores or Greats (classics), 1878

Edwin Hubble, MA in Jurisprudence, Literature and Spanish, 1913

T. S. Eliot, BA in Philosophy, 1914

J. R. R. Tolkien, BA in English Literature, 1915

Aldous Huxley, BA in English Literature, 1916

Margaret Thatcher, BA in Chemistry, 1947

Stephen Hawking, a BA degree in Physics, 1962

Rowan Atkinson, MSc in Electrical Engineering, 1975

Tony Blair, BA in Jurisprudence, 1975

Sir Tim Berners-Lee, BA in Physics, 1975

Hugh Grant, BA in English, 1982

David Cameron, BA in Philosophy, Politics and Economics, 1988

"Oh, Moneypenny. I'm just up here at Oxford, brushing up on a little Danish."

James Bond, to Moneypenny, after Bond "visits" Professor Inga Bergstrom at Oxford University's New College, *Tomorrow Never Dies*, 1997

21 July 1888

The date that *Jackson's Oxford Journal* published a list of all the executions that had taken place in Oxford during the previous century. In total, 44 men were hanged for burglary, horse theft, highway robbery, arson and sheep stealing. After 1836, only murderers were executed.

Under the Murder Act of 1752, a person convicted of murder in Oxford had to hanged publicly within 48 hours and the corpse remain "hanging in chains", an act known as gibbeting, so as to deter others from committing such a heinous crime.

"There are few greater temptations on Earth than to stay permanently at Oxford in meditation, and to read all the books in the Bodleian."

Hilaire Belloc, 1902

22 Northmoor Road

The family address of Oxford's most revered fantasist, J. R. R. Tolkien, author of the classics *The Hobbit* (1937) and *The Lord of the Rings* (1954). Famously, Tolkien wrote the memorable first line of *The Hobbit* – "In a hole in the ground there lived a hobbit" – while marking exam papers for students during his tenure as Professor of English Language and Literature at Oxford University.

In 1945, after twenty years at Pembroke College, Tolkien moved to Merton College. It was while here that he wrote *The Lord of the Rings*. He had been a student at Exeter College, graduating in 1915 after having started at Oxford in 1911, aged 19.

"Oxford is on the
whole more attractive
than Cambridge to the
ordinary visitor; and the
traveller is therefore
recommended to visit
Cambridge first, or to
omit it altogether if
he cannot visit both."

Karl Baedeker, *Great Britain*, 1887

"We filmed the video for 'Creep' at The Jericho in 1992, playing two shows: the morning one was an all-ages show with 11-year-olds pogoing and their parents stood against the wall waiting for them to go home, and the later show in the evening had an older crowd. We went on a US tour after that video came out. As it was on heavy rotation, it felt like everywhere we went there was a little bit of Oxford with us."

Colin Greenwood, of the band Radiohead, on Oxford's beloved 1990s music venue, The Jericho, *Guardian*, January 2014

It Belongs in a Museum

Beaumont Street's Ashmolean Museum, named after its founder Elias Ashmole, opened in 1683. It is regarded as the world's first modern public museum and the world's first university museum. It is home to more than one million items of history, ranging from priceless masterpieces to ancient jewels, archaeological treasures to stunning sculptures and statues.

The most famous pieces currently housed in the museum are perhaps *The Hunt in the Forest* (1470) by Paolo Uccello, the ninth-century Alfred Jewel, the Ancient Egyptian statue of Sobek, the crocodile god, and *St John the Baptist* (1513) by Leonardo da Vinci. The museum closes at 5 p.m., so what are you waiting for?

The Bodleian Library

Established in 1602, Oxford's Bodleian Library – named after the scholar Thomas Bodley – is one of the oldest libraries and research centres in Europe and the second largest library in the UK (after the British Library).

The hallowed halls of the Bod, as it is known in Oxford slang, contain more than 13 million books – and counting! – which take up more than 240 kilometres (150 miles) of shelving. In fact, the newest additions to the library add an extra 5 kilometres (3 miles) of shelving *every year*. That's not including the 300 terabytes of data stored online, a number that will jump to a petabyte, or 1 million gigabytes, in the next few years. To store this amount of data at home, you would need to print a book 500 billion pages long!

The Bodleian Library has the right to request a free copy of every book published in the UK – more than 200,000 a year – and it reserves the right never to lend books, even to royalty. Charles I discovered this in 1645 when he asked to borrow a book – a world history by French poet Agrippa d'Aubigné – but the librarian said no.

"This Oxford, I have no doubt is the finest city in the world."

John Keats, in a letter he wrote to his sister Fanny, 10 September 1817

A Glass of Sherry

According to the *Grey Book*, a centuries-old tome that contains all of the university's examination regulations – it's now all online, of course – there is a stipulation that if a student arrives at the Exam Schools (where all university exams take place) on a horse, in full armour and carrying a sword, then examiners must give the student a glass of sherry.

Try it – what's the worst that could happen?

Punting

"Beware of men who offer to go in a punt with you; such men will not help you except by their countenance, but will occupy the cushions."

Oxford Spectator, Tuesday, 21 April 1868

Along with cycling, punting is today one of Oxford's best-loved leisure activities and a boating tradition that dates back to 1860. Punting is best enjoyed between March and October and, on a warm, cloudless, summery day, thousands of punters and their passengers can be seen floating leisurely down the River Cherwell.

While in Cambridge, the punter stands on the till, the raised platform, pushing the boat with the open end facing forwards, in Oxford, the punter stands inside the punt with the till end facing forwards.

High Street, Oxford

"My job is to paint what
I see, not what I know."

J. M. W. Turner, as quoted in *A Poet's Journal: Days of 1945–1951*, by George Seferis, 1999

One of the most celebrated art masterpieces, perhaps of all time, is English romantic painter J. M. W. Turner's *High Street, Oxford* (1810). Turner is regarded as one of the greatest landscape artists of all time and is often called the "Painter of Light" because of his expressive use of colouring. *High Street, Oxford*, which depicts two of the city's dreaming spires – can you name them? – and a bustling city centre, is available to visit and view at the Ashmolean Museum on Beaumont Street.

"Ye sacred nurseries of blooming youth!
In whose collegiate shelter England's
flowers
Expand, enjoying through their vernal
hours
The air of liberty, the light of truth;
Much have ye suffered from Time's
gnawing tooth,
Yet, O ye spires of Oxford! domes
and towers!
Gardens and groves! your presence
overpowers"

William Wordsworth, from "Oxford", 30 May 1820

Sister Cities

Oxford is one of the leading cities in the UK for twinning, a process that became popular after the Second World War to encourage two towns or cities in different countries to form a cultural bond. Oxford is twinned with:

1. **Leiden**, Netherlands – since 1946
2. **Bonn**, Germany – since 1947
3. **León**, Nicaragua – since 1986
4. **Grenoble**, France – since 1989
5. **Wrocław**, Poland – since 2018
6. **Ramallah**, Palestine – since 2019
7. **Padua**, Italy – since 2019

Though not an official twin, the city of **Oxford**, Mississippi, in the United States was founded in 1837. It was named after Oxford, England, in the hope that it would one day become a university town. It is home to Mississippi's state university, which was founded in 1848.

Oxford Terms

An undergraduate's year at Oxford University is divided into three terms:

Michaelmas

The first, or autumn, term
(October to December)

Hilary

The second, or spring, term
(January to March)

Trinity

The third, or summer, term
(April to June)

"To call a man a characteristically Oxford man is, in my opinion, to give him the highest compliment that could be paid to any human being."

William Gladstone, in a speech to the Oxford Union, February 1890

Oxford

"I speak not of this college or of that, but of the university as a whole; and, gentlemen, what a whole Oxford is!"

John Coleridge, in *Collections and Recollections*, by George William Erskine Russell, Harper & Brothers, 1898

"The world surely has not
another place like Oxford;
it is a despair to see such a
place and ever to leave it,
for it would take a lifetime
and more than one to
comprehend and enjoy
it satisfactorily."

Nathaniel Hawthorne, *Passages from the English Note-books*, Volume II, 1804

4 University Challenge

"I wonder anybody does anything at Oxford but dream and remember, the place is so beautiful. One almost expects the people to sing instead of speaking. It is all like an opera."

William Butler Yeats, in a letter to Katharine Tynan, 1888

Brideshead Revisited

"Oxford, in those days, was still a city of aquatint. In her spacious and quiet streets men walked and spoke as they had done in Newman's day; her autumnal mists, her grey springtime, and the rare glory of her summer days – such as that day – when the chestnut was in flower and the bells rang out high and clear over her gables and cupolas, exhaled the soft airs of centuries of youth."

Evelyn Waugh, *Brideshead Revisited*, 1945

Evelyn Waugh's classic British novel, *Brideshead Revisited*, is one of the most admired works of fiction set, at least in part, in Oxford. The plot follows protagonist Charles Ryder, an Oxford University history undergraduate as he befriends – and possibly more – the flamboyant, wealthy, but troubled, Lord Sebastian Flyte and his group of friends. Today, *Brideshead Revisited* is a classic, and often voted as one of the 100 best books of world literature.

The OED

The most comprehensive record of the English language on Earth, the *Oxford English Dictionary* (OED) was first published in 1884 and stands proud as a national treasure and international icon, with at least one copy (in the attic) in every household in Britain. Today, the OED is home to more than 600,000 words!*

The OED first began cataloguing the English Language in 1857, but the process was so thorough that it took *four years* to get from A to ... Ant. Indeed, beloved Oxford academic and resident J. R. R. Tolkien contributed to the "W" section of the dictionary ... in 1928!

An educated Oxford student "only" knows around 50,000 words, though the average is around 30,000 in Britain. It is estimated that an average human being speaks around 800 million words in their lifetime.

Stephen Hawking

"If you award me a First, I will go to Cambridge. If I receive a Second, I shall stay in Oxford, so I expect you will give me a First."

Stephen Hawking, "A Brief History of Mine" speech, Cambridge Union, November 2017

Stephen Hawking, the genius theoretical physicist, was a student of both Oxford and Cambridge. It is his legendary student days at University College, Oxford, in the 1960s that are recalled, however, in the biographical, Oscar-winning *The Theory of Everything*, starring Eddie Redmayne and Felicity Jones, released in 2014.

At Oxford, Hawking considered himself to be a "lazy and difficult" student who found exams "ridiculously easy", but lacked the discipline to study. "At Oxford you were supposed to be brilliant without effort or accept your limitations and get a fourth-class degree," he once said. It was in 1974 that Hawking had his black hole breakthrough and became a worldwide scientist-celebrity. In 1978, he received the Albert Einstein Medal and an honorary doctorate from Oxford.

"By the cut of your suit, you went to Oxford. Naturally you think human beings dress like that. But you wear it with such disdain, my guess is you didn't come from money, and your school friends never let you forget it. Which means you were at that school by the grace of someone else's charity – hence that chip on your shoulder."

Vesper Lynd, analyzing the spy James Bond as a means to taunt him, *Casino Royale*, 2006

"I saw the spires of Oxford
As I was passing by,
The grey spires of Oxford
Against a pearl-grey sky;
My heart was with the Oxford men
Who went abroad to die."

Winifred Mary Letts, "The Spires of Oxford", 1916

Fictional Graduates

It isn't just real people who have made a name for themselves after leaving Oxford University. A few fictional characters have studied there too and gone on to be quite successful in their chosen fields.

1. **Frasier Crane** – *Frasier*
2. **Jay Gatsby** – *The Great Gatsby*
3. **Captain Hook** – *Peter Pan*
4. **Fox Mulder** – *The X-Files*
5. **George Smiley** – John le Carré's spymaster
6. **Bertie Wooster** – P. G. Wodehouse's amiable English gentleman
7. **Charles Xavier** – the leader of the X-Men in the Marvel comics
8. **Henry Jones** – the father of Indiana Jones
9. **Raj Koothrappali** – a character in *The Big Bang Theory* who has a doctorate in astrophysics
10. **Thomas Crown** – the rich playboy art thief in *The Thomas Crown Affair*

World's First Antibiotic

The University of Oxford has been at the forefront of scientific innovations and inventions since its earliest days. Countless discoveries are made each year in Oxford's colleges and laboratories. However, few have had more impact than Sir Howard Florey's development of penicillin in the 1940s, the world's very first antibiotic. Florey's work with his team at Oxford has saved an estimated 500 million lives worldwide.

While Alexander Fleming, with whom Florey shares the 1945 Nobel Prize for medicine, receives most of the credit for discovering penicillin, it was Florey's work at Oxford, pioneering clinical trials, that led to the mass production of penicillin as a miracle cure for bacterial infections.

"Oxford lends sweetness to labour and dignity to leisure."

Henry James, as quoted in *Oxford in Quotations*, University of Chicago Press, 2014

"Sir, if a man has a mind
to prance, he must study at
Christ Church and All Souls."

Samuel Johnson, as quoted in James Boswell,
Life of Samuel Johnson, LL.D., Vol. II, 1791

BOP Till You Drop

BOPs, or Big Open Parties, are a regular event for students of any one of Oxford University's colleges, and a quintessential part of the university experience. BOPs are usually themed costume parties organized by individual colleges at several times throughout the three terms. Held in the college bars, the BOPs have become (in)famous, with students encouraged to create their own fancy dress.

Dinosaurs

Fifteen years before the coining of the word "dinosaur" in 1841 by Richard Owens, Corpus Christi student William Buckland minted the term Megalosaurus, meaning "great lizard". Buckland's discovery was the first "dinosaur" to be named – and even takes the scientific name of *M. bucklandii*, after its discoverer – and is the basis for Richard Owen's future classification.

Buckland was also known as "Oxford's most eccentric man" as he often took his work home with him. His dining-room table was inlaid with dinosaur poop; he would often eat creatures he researched – anything from crocodile to panther, mouse to mole, and even ate a portion of the mummified heart of King Louis XIV. To some, Buckland was a genius. Others, like Charles Darwin, considered him "a buffoon".

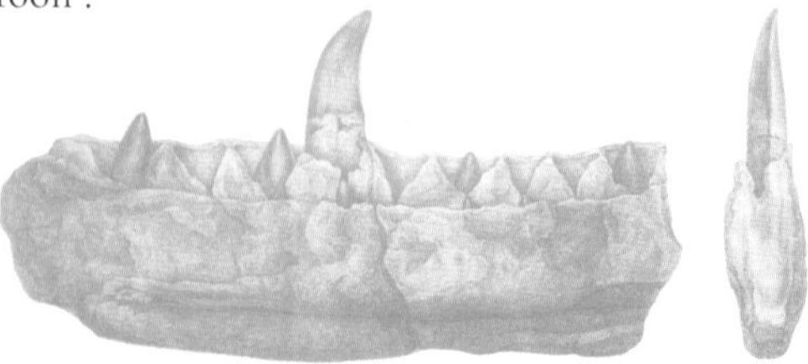

From William Buckland's *Notice on the Megalosaurus or Great Fossil Lizard of Stonesfield*: "Anterior extremity of the right lower jaw of the Megalosaurus. From Stonesfield, near Oxford."

"Oxford is so beautiful
still that only those who
know her history are
sensible of any loss."

E. A. Greening Lamborn, *The Story of Architecture in Oxford Stone*, 1912

Oxford Wordplay

Did you know, from the word "Oxford", you can make the following 12 words:

Inspector Morse

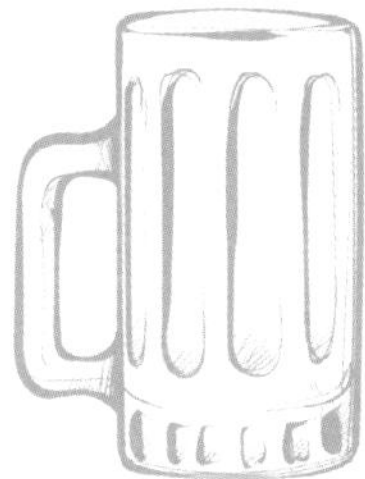

One of Britain's best-loved fictional detective characters, Inspector Endeavour Morse, created by Oxford resident Colin Dexter, famously solved grisly crimes in and around the city from 1987 to 2000 in the 33-episode hit ITV series that became synonymous with the city and was filmed at many of the city's most iconic sites. Across Dexter's 13 *Inspector Morse* titles, the author calculated that he had murdered 81 Oxonians, each one a puzzle for Morse to solve, and making Oxford one of the highest murder capitals of the world – again! (See Medieval Murder Capital on p. 12.)

Oxford Botanic Garden

Founded at precisely 2 o'clock on Sunday, 25 July 1621, Oxford University's Botanic Garden is the oldest and biggest botanic garden in Britain, home to more than 5,000 different plant species and, in its herbaria, more than 1 million specimens of plant seeds.

The garden is also famous as a literary landmark. Oxford professor and author, J. R. R. Tolkien, regularly visited the garden and always sat under his favourite tree, *Pinus nigra*. This supremely tall Austrian pine was the inspiration for Tolkien's Ents, the slow but powerful tree-people of Middle Earth in *The Lord of the Rings*.

May the First Be With You

May the First in Oxford is a very special day indeed. Known locally as May Morning, this annual, traditional celebration to welcome the start of spring dates back more than 500 years. The day starts at 6 a.m. with tens of thousands* of Oxonians gathering below Magdalen Tower to hear the Magdalen College Choir sing "Hymnus Eucharisticus" and "Now is the Month of Maying". Afterwards, the crowds head to Radcliffe Square and revel in Morris dancing, live music and a party atmosphere that continues well into the evening.

*The record to date is 27,000.

The Seven Wonders of Oxford

Oxford has scores of world-class and world-famous landmarks and listed buildings, including the outstanding architecture of the 39 college buildings. Should you be in a hurry on your visit to the city, may we recommend the "Seven Wonders of Oxford", a must-see list to celebrate the city's most significant architectural attractions:

1. The Radcliffe Camera
2. The Sheldonian Theatre
3. The Bridge of Sighs
4. The Bodleian Library
5. Oxford Castle and Prison
6. Christ Church
7. Carfax Tower

The Radcliffe Camera – from the Latin *camera*, meaning "room" – is Oxford's stand-out building. Designed by James Gibbs in the baroque style and built between 1737 and 1749, the Radcliffe Camera was Britain's first circular library. Tolkien cited the circular architecture as his inspiration for the Dark Lord Sauron's temple in *The Lord of the Rings*.

Nobel Laureates

Oxford University has not only nurtured more philosophers, poets and physicists than anywhere else in the world, it has also produced the most Nobel Prize winners – more than 70 of them!

Nobel Prizes have been awarded every year since 1895 and are, of course, among the most prestigious awards in the world. They are awarded to people whose life's work has delivered the greatest benefit to humankind. These names should ring a bell:

1. **Sir Howard Walter Florey** (Physiology or Medicine, 1945)
2. **Erwin Schrödinger** (Physics, 1933)
3. **Peter Higgs** (Physics, 2013)
4. **Dorothy Crowfoot Hodgkin** (Chemistry, 1964)
5. **T. S. Eliot** (Literature, 1948)
6. **Kazuo Ishiguro** (Literature, 2017)
7. **Malala Yousafzai** (Peace, 2014)
8. **Albert Schweitzer** (Peace, 1952)
9. **Sir Roger Penrose** (Physics, 2020)
10. **Elinor Ostrom** (Economic Sciences, 2009)

The University of Harry Potter

With its ancient and aesthetically arresting architecture, Oxford is one of the most photographed cities in the world, and a popular film location for Hollywood blockbusters. Its most celebrated movie connection is perhaps the Harry Potter* franchise.

When not drinking in the Turf Tavern, the cast of the magical seven-film series could be seen whipping their wands out around Oxford, including the Bodley Staircase and the cloisters at Christ Church, and the Bodleian Library; the Great Dining Hall at Christ Church also provided the inspiration for the dining hall at Hogwarts.

*FYI, Emma Watson auditioned for the role of Hermione Granger while she was a pupil at Oxford's prestigious Dragon School, aged just ten.

The Turf Tavern

Oxford's most famous pub has to be one of its oldest, the Turf Tavern! This venue's history reaches all the way back to 1381 when it was known as the Spotted Cow, a name it kept until 1842. Tucked away down a dark, narrow alley, once known as "Hell's Passage", the Turf, with its low, wooden beams, has been the place to drink and smoke for many esteemed world figures and Oxford undergrads, including physicist Stephen Hawking, C. S. Lewis, Margaret Thatcher, Tony Blair, Elizabeth Taylor and Richard Burton. It was, according to legend, also the pub where former US President Bill Clinton, while a student at Oxford, notoriously smoked marijuana. "When I was in England I experimented with marijuana a time or two, and I didn't like it. I didn't inhale it, and never tried it again," he said, to much ridicule from the media.

The Bridge of Sighs

The Bridge of Sighs is a beloved, 500-year old landmark in a truly iconic City of Bridges, 435 of them – Venice. In Italy, the Bridge of Sighs is an arched crossing that connects Prigioni Nuove (New Prison) to the Doge's Palace. The bridge's English name was given to it by Lord Byron because of his belief that prisoners would sigh one last time at the view of beautiful Venice through the bridge's window before being locked in their cells.

Oxford, too, has a Bridge of Sighs, which is twinned with the Venetian one. The bridge in Oxford connects the northern and southern parts of Hertford College. It is one of the seven wonders of Oxford. One can imagine Jonathan Swift, author of *Gulliver's Travels*, conjuring up images of Lilliput as he crossed the bridge.

The Oxford Comma

Grammatically offensive to some, the Oxford comma is a comma placed after the second to last item in a sentence. For example, there is no Oxford comma in this sentence taken from a caption to a photograph illustrating an article about a documentary on American singer-songwriter Merle Haggard: "Among those interviewed were his two ex-wives, Kris Kristofferson and Robert Duvall," which appears to suggest that Merle was married to the two men, which he wasn't. "Among those interviewed were his two ex-wives, Kris Kristofferson, and Robert Duvall," would read more clearly.

Also known as the serial comma, it is called the "Oxford comma" because it is the preferred grammatical style of the Oxford University Press.

,

The Oxfordian Theory

While there are several conspiracy theories as to who really authored the works of William Shakespeare (other than the great man himself, of course) the most popular alternative train of thought is known as the Oxfordian Theory.

In 1920, J. Thomas Looney,* an English schoolmaster, published a book that claimed Edward de Vere, the 17th Earl of Oxford, was in fact the *real* bard. Historians and literary scholars, many of them Oxford heavyweights, overwhelmingly dismissed Looney's claim. However, a century later, the conspiracy lives on, even going so far as to inspire the 2011 Hollywood drama, *Anonymous*, starring Rhys Ifans.

*Nominative determinism at its best.

"I remember very well,
when I was at Oxford, an
old gentleman said to me,
'Young man, ply your book
diligently now, and acquire
a stock of knowledge; for
when years come upon you,
you will find that poring
upon books will be but
an irksome task."

Samuel Johnson, as quoted in James Boswell,
Life of Samuel Johnson, LL.D., Vol. I, 1791

Picture Credits

Wikimedia Commons: David Iliff (Licence: CC BY-SA3.0), 3; Morris, Tasker & Co., 10; Balon Greyjoy, 17; Jonathan Bowen, 18; 20; ALC Washingon, 23; Steve Jurvetson, 26; Motacilla, 33; James Tissot, 34; St Anne's College, Oxford University, 42; Bibliothéque nationale de France, 47; Napoleon Sarony, 50; Ronan Munro, 51; John Speed, 52–53; Metropolitan Museum of Art, 54; Wellcome Images, 56, 87; Metropolitan Museum of Art, 59; Jonas Magnus Lystad, 62; Nightstallion, 68; decltype, 73; Hogweard, 74; Motacilla, 76; Ozeye, 78; Adrian Hon, 79; Jpbowen, 84; Julian Smith, 110; Mary Morland, 114; 119; Bridge of Sighs David Hallam-Jones/Hertford Bridge, often called the Bridge of Sighs, Oxford/CC BY-SA 2.0, 124. Shutterstock: Map Graphic Resources, 4; Art Studio VN, 7; Greens87, 31; Chris Bain, 43; antonpix, 98. thegraphicsfairy.com: 8, 90, 122. Freepik: inksyndromeartwork, 12; rawpixel.com, 15, 28, 72, 126; pikisuperstar, 30; freepik, 32, 117. Alamy Stock Photo: PjrTravel, 61; Quagga Media, 118